# DELTADROMEUS

## AND OTHER SHORELINE DINOSAURS

by **Dougal Dixon**

illustrated by
**Steve Weston** and **James Field**

PICTURE WINDOW BOOKS
Minneapolis, Minnesota

Picture Window Books
5115 Excelsior Boulevard
Suite 232
Minneapolis, MN 55416
877-845-8392
www.picturewindowbooks.com

Printed in the United States of America.

**Library of Congress Cataloging-in-Publication Data**
Dixon, Dougal.
Deltadromeus and other shoreline dinosaurs / written
by Dougal Dixon ; illustrations by James Field, Steve
Weston ; diagrams by Stefan Chabluk ; cover art by
Steve Weston.
p. cm. — (Dinosaur find)
Includes bibliographical references and index.
ISBN 1-4048-0669-5
1. Dinosaurs—Juvenile literature. 2. Seashore
animals—Juvenile literature. I. Field, James, 1959- ill.
II. Weston, Steve, ill. III. Chabluk, Stefan, ill. IV. Title.
QE861.5.D583 2005
567.9–dc22                            2004007306

**Acknowledgments**
This book was produced for Picture Window Books
by Bender Richardson White, U.K.

Illustrations by James Field (pages 4–5, 9, 11, 13, 15)
and Steve Weston (cover and pages 7, 17, 19, 21).
Diagrams by Stefan Chabluk.
All photographs copyright Digital Vision except
page 6 (Corbis Images, Inc.).

Consultant: John Stidworthy, Scientific Fellow of
the Zoological Society, London, and former
Lecturer in the Education Department, Natural
History Museum, London.

Reading Adviser: Rosemary G. Palmer, Ph.D.,
Department of Literacy, College of Education,
Boise State University, Idaho.

**Types of dinosaurs**
In this book, a red shape at the
top of a left-hand page shows
the animal was a meat-eater.
A green shape shows it was
a plant-eater.

**Just how big—or small—
were they?**
Dinosaurs were many different
sizes. We have compared their
size to one of the following:

Chicken
2 feet (60 cm) tall
Weight 6 pounds (2.7 kg)

Adult person
6 feet (1.8 m) tall
Weight 170 pounds (76.5 kg)

Elephant
10 feet (3 m) tall
Weight 12,000 pounds
(5,400 kg)

# TABLE OF CONTENTS

# WHAT'S INSIDE?

Dinosaurs! These dinosaurs lived near seashores, lakes, and riverbanks. Find out how they survived millions of years ago and what they have in common with today's animals.

# Life Near the Sea

Dinosaurs lived between 230 million and 65 million years ago. The world did not look the same then. The land and seas were not in the same places. Many dinosaurs lived on beaches and riverbanks. They found a lot of things to eat near the water.

Meat-eating dinosaur *Deltadromeus* hunted plant-eaters such as the long-necked *Paralititan*. *Suchomimus* fished in the shallow water. Sea reptiles swam in the water and were sometimes washed up on the beach.

5

# COMPSOGNATHUS

Pronunciation:
KOMP-sog-NAY-thus

Tiny *Compsognathus* had long, strong legs. It could run quickly back and forth in shallow water. It hunted insects, small seashore animals, and lizards. It caught them with its sharp, little teeth.

## The chase today

Herons have long legs like *Compsognathus* did. Herons also look in shallow water for animals to eat.

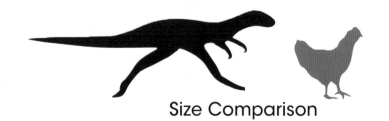

Size Comparison

A *Compsognathus* sprinted along the shore chasing a lizard. If it caught the lizard, it would swallow it whole.

*Corythosaurus* used its beak to scoop up plants from the bottom of the swamp. It had a bump on its nose. The bump had air tubes inside. It might have been used to call to other dinosaurs or to help smell things.

### Cooling off today

Hippopotamuses cool off in the water like *Corythosaurus* did long ago.

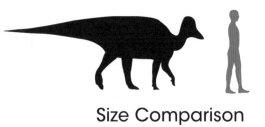

Size Comparison

*Corythosaurus* would soak in the forest swamp to cool off.

9

# MASIAKASAURUS

Pronunciation:
MAS-ee-ah-ka-SAW-rus

*Masiakasaurus* teeth made a perfect fish trap. The teeth were spiky and had hooked tips. The dinosaur could snap its long jaws at a fish. Crunch!

**Spiky teeth today**

The rare gharial crocodiles of India have spiky fish-catching teeth like *Masiakasaurus* did.

Size Comparison

A *Masiakasaurus* stood in a jungle stream. As a fish swam by, the dinosaur dipped its head. Snap! It caught a meal.

# PARALITITAN

Pronunciation:
PAR-uh-lee-TYE-tan

*Paralititan* traveled in herds. They wandered across mud flats looking for plants to eat. Their huge flat feet were perfectly shaped for mud walking. They kept *Paralititan* from slipping or sinking.

### Flat feet today

Wide feet help camels stay on top of desert sand. Camels move in herds like *Paralititan* did millions of years ago.

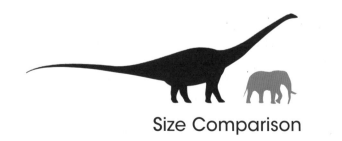

Size Comparison

*Paralititan* were always on the move looking for food.

# PELECANIMIMUS

*Pelecanimimus* grabbed a fish in its jaws and lifted its head out of the water. The fish fell into the pouch under the dinosaur's chin. *Pelecanimimus* held the fish in the pouch before gulping it down.

**Food pouch today**

A pelican has a pouch like *Pelecanimimus* did. Its pouch can hold several fish at a time.

Size Comparison

16

*Pelecanimimus* searched a rock pool for fish and shrimp.

# STRUTHIOSAURUS

Pronunciation: STROO-thee-o-SAW-rus

There is not much to eat on an island, so *Struthiosaurus* ate any plants it found. It was a small armored dinosaur. It would have made a good meal for the island's meat-eaters.

## Island life today

The Galapagos tortoise is the largest tortoise. It lives on islands like *Struthiosaurus* did long ago.

Size Comparison

A *Struthiosaurus* would quietly move through the ferns sniffing out plants to eat. It did not want to become a meal itself.

# SUCHOMIMUS

Pronunciation:
SOO-cho-MYE-mus

*Suchomimus* had huge thumb claws. It used them to stab fish in the water. Then it flipped the fish into its jaws. *Suchomimus* may also have been a good swimmer. Its strong back legs and tail could help it swim.

**Going fishing today**

Grizzly bears use their claws to catch fish like *Suchomimus* once did.

Size Comparison

*Suchomimus* hunted for fish in the river. When they saw some, whack! Then the dinosaurs crunched the fish in their long crocodilelike jaws.

# WHERE DID THEY GO?

Dinosaurs are extinct, which means that none of them are alive today. Scientists study rocks and fossils to find clues about what happened to dinosaurs.

People have different explanations about what happened. Some people think a huge asteroid that hit Earth caused all sorts of climate changes. This then caused the dinosaurs to die. Others think volcanic eruptions caused the climate to change and that killed the dinosaurs. No one knows for sure, though.

# GLOSSARY

**armor**—a protective covering of plates or horns, spikes, or clubs used for fighting

**beak**—the hard front part of the mouth of birds and some dinosaurs

**ferns**—plants with finely divided leaves known as fronds; ferns are common in damp woods and along rivers

**herds**—large groups of animals that move, feed, and sleep together

**reptile**—a cold-blooded animal with a backbone and scales; it walks on short legs or crawls on its belly

**rock pools**—hollows between rocks on a beach that are filled with seawater and often contain small fish, crabs, anemones, and seaweed

# FIND OUT MORE

## AT THE LIBRARY

Dixon, Dougal. *Dinosaurs: The Good, the Bad, and the Ugly*. New York: Dorling Kindersley, 2001.

Lessem, Don. *The Fastest Dinosaurs*. Minneapolis: Lerner, 2005.

Muehlenhardt, Amy Bailey. *Drawing and Learning About Dinosaurs*. Minneapolis: Picture Window Books, 2004.

## ON THE WEB

FactHound offers a safe, fun way to find Web sites related to this book. All of the sites on FactHound have been researched by our staff.
*www.facthound.com*

1. Visit the FactHound home page.

2. Enter a search word related to this book, or type in this special code: 1404806695.

3. Click on the Fetch It button.

Your trusty FactHound will fetch the best Web sites for you!

# INDEX